Nonprofit Quick Guide™

How to Involve Volunteers in Your Fundraising Program

Linda Lysakowski, ACFRE
Joanne Oppelt, MHA

Nonprofit Quick Guide: How to Involve Volunteers in Your Fundraising Program

One of the **Nonprofit Quick Guide**™ series

Published by Joanne Oppelt Consulting, LLC

ISBN Print Book: 978-1-951978-06-8

13 12 11 10 9 8 7 6 5 4 3 2 1

About the Authors

LINDA LYSAKOWSKI, ACFRE

Linda is one of approximately one hundred professionals worldwide to hold the Advanced Certified Fundraising Executive designation. Linda is the author of ten nonfiction books, a contributing author, co-editor, or coauthor of twenty-four others. She has also written six books unrelated to the nonprofit world.

Linda has more than thirty years in the development field. She worked for a university and a museum before starting her own consulting firm. In her twenty-five years as a philanthropic consultant, Linda has managed capital campaigns that have raised more than $50 million, helped hundreds of nonprofit organizations achieve their development goals, and trained more than forty thousand development professionals in most of the fifty states of the United States, Canada, Mexico, Egypt, and Bermuda.

She served on the Association of Fundraising Philanthropy (AFP) Foundation for Philanthropy Board and on the Professional Advancement Division for AFP. She is a past president of the Eastern Pennsylvania and Sierra (Nevada) AFP chapters. She received the Outstanding Fundraiser of the Year award from the Eastern Pennsylvania, Las Vegas, and Sierra (Nevada) chapters of AFP, was honored with the Barbara Marion Award for Outstanding Service to AFP, and received the Lifetime Achievement Award from the Las Vegas AFP chapter.

Linda is a graduate of Alvernia University with majors in banking and finance as well as theology/philosophy, and a minor in communications. As a graduate of AFP's Faculty Training Academy, she is a Master Teacher.

JOANNE OPPELT, MHA

Joanne, principal of Joanne Oppelt Consulting, LLC, is a seasoned rainmaker with a distinguished track record of success. During her twenty-five-plus years working in the nonprofit arena, she built or rebuilt successful fundraising departments at every stop, helping her organizations grow capacity and more effectively fulfill their missions.

She has held positions from grant writer to executive director at the nonprofits Community Access Unlimited, Caring Contact: A Listening Community, Family to Family Network of New Jersey, Christian Healthcare Center, March of Dimes Central New Jersey, Prevent Child Abuse New Jersey, and Maternal and Family Health Services. Her extensive background in a variety of work roles and organizations enables her to understand the realities and challenges nonprofit practitioners face—both internally and externally. Her success at every stop positions her to help any nonprofit, whether through her books or consulting practice, turn around its struggling fundraising operations.

Joanne is the author of four books and coauthor of twelve. She has taught at Kean University as an Adjunct Professor in its graduate program. She is also a highly sought-after speaker and presenter.

Joanne holds a master's degree in health administration from Wilkes University, where she graduated with distinction. Her bachelor's degree is in education, with a minor in psychology.

Dedication

This book is dedicated to the enthusiastic and hard-working volunteers who have enabled nonprofits to raise millions of dollars through their support and dedication.

Contents

Chapter One

Expanding Your View of Volunteers in Fundraising

Your organization may already use volunteers in your program activities and/or to help with clerical work, but you can also involve volunteers in your fundraising program. Volunteers can play a critical role in fundraising, working along with the board and staff. The key is learning how to recruit the right volunteers for the right job and provide these volunteers with the tools they need to be effective fundraisers.

Volunteers can be some of the best advocates for your organization. Your ability to recruit volunteer fundraisers can help lend credibility among your constituents by showing that community members are enthusiastic about and committed to your organization.

Some Key Concepts for Involving Volunteers as Fundraisers

- Volunteers will be effective only if they honestly believe in the mission of your organization.
- Volunteers should be invited to give of their time, talent, and treasure.
- Volunteers must be given meaningful work, not just "busy work."
- Volunteers require staff support to be effective.

As with donors, volunteers will become involved in your organization for many reasons, including their own family history, religious influence, altruism, wanting to give back, community spirit, investing in their own or someone else's future, or because it is fun. If they do not believe in your mission, however, they will not be effective fundraising volunteers.

One question that often comes up is, "Do we ask volunteers to also give financially? They are giving their time, and we don't want to also ask them to make a financial donation." You have probably heard this from some of your key volunteers—board members. We could put it bluntly and say, while time is great, you cannot take it to the bank and deposit it. But there is a much more positive way to think about this issue. Think about your own charitable giving. Like you, we are busy people and do not have a lot of time to volunteer. But we do have our favorite causes for which we find the time. Linda often says she has two organizations for which she makes time to volunteer—her church and its outreach ministries, and the Association of Fundraising Professionals. She says when she does her taxes at the end of the year, who gets the most charitable contributions from her? Her church and AFP! So, if people are passionate enough to give you their time, they will most likely also give when they are asked to contribute financially.

Linda did research several years ago when she wrote her first book on this topic and recalls an interesting response at one of her focus groups. She asked attendees how they felt about being asked for financial contributions from organizations for which they volunteered. Not one person said they objected to being asked. However, one gentleman reported that he was unhappy when an organization for which he had volunteered over many years sent him a "Dear Friend" letter asking for support, with no reference to the fact that he was a valued volunteer.

So, if you are soliciting your volunteers for financial gifts, make sure you recognize their contributions of time and thank them for their commitment to your organization before you ask. And, we do recommend that you ask volunteers to support you financially. According to Volunteer Hub, volunteers are 66 percent more likely to give monetarily to the organizations they volunteer for than those who do not volunteer.

Fundraising Roles for Volunteers

Many times, when we ask people if they involve volunteers in their fundraising efforts, the answers are things like using volunteers for special events, stuffing envelopes, and the like. However, there are a lot of ways you can involve volunteers in your fundraising activities beyond those ways mentioned, so we want you to think outside the box. Each of these fundraising methods will be discussed in more detail in future chapters. However, let us start thinking about how volunteers can be useful in each of these areas. Following are some of the activities volunteers can help with:

◆ Research
◆ Planning
◆ Special events
◆ Direct mail

◆ Telephone fundraising

◆ Business appeals

◆ Major gifts appeals

◆ Capital and endowment campaigns

◆ Planned giving efforts

You can involve volunteers in every aspect of your fundraising effort, starting with your annual fund. Having a volunteer chair or co-chair for your annual fund encompasses all your fundraising efforts for the year—direct mail, telephone appeals, major gifts, and any efforts that don't already have a formal chairperson. This can lend special credibility when approaching donors. The annual fund chair will create a special importance for your overall appeal, which might include a business appeal, a major gift effort, a phonathon, a direct mail campaign, and special events. All these segments of your annual fund can effectively use volunteers, and each should have its own chair and committee of volunteers.

Wrapping It Up

◆ Think outside the box when it comes to involving volunteers in your fundraising activities.

◆ Volunteers want meaningful work.

◆ Do ask your volunteers for financial support, especially when they will be asking others for money.

◆ Volunteers will be more successful if they care about your mission.

Chapter Two

Involving Volunteers in Research and Planning

Volunteers can be helpful in doing research, especially if they are detail-oriented and computer savvy. They can help research foundations, businesses, and individuals.

Foundations

Staff members usually prepare grant proposals, except in exceedingly small organizations that have no staff. Volunteers might then step in to fill this role. Be extremely cautious about having volunteers write grant proposals unless they are experienced professionals. Writing successful proposals takes a lot of skill and training; not just anyone can write a good grant. And you need to be careful in how your nonprofit comes across to funders. Funders are a small group, and your agency's reputation will get around. You don't want a reputation for being unprofessional; however, researching foundations could be a very productive role and save you tons of time.

Suppose you have access to the Foundation Directory, Foundation Search, or other foundation research tools. In that case, a good volunteer can search for foundations that might be a good match for your organization's programs and projects. You can also show volunteers how to use GuideStar to search the IRS 990PF forms of foundations to find out more about the types of organizations they fund, the types of projects they are interested in, and the amount of the foundation's typical grants.

Also, proposals to foundations need that personal touch. One way to give volunteers a meaningful part in your grant fundraising is to review the list of potential grant funders with your development committee or your board members or other volunteers to determine if they have any personal contacts with foundation trustees. You should develop a list of the foundations you plan to approach with the foundations' trustees and other information about the foundation. Asking volunteers to review this list and identify any trustees they have personal contact with will help you develop a personalized appeal. Volunteers can also be invited to attend meetings with potential funders to help add credibility to your organization and speak to the funders from the point of view of a volunteer who has committed time and money to the organization.

If you do know a foundation board member, though, make sure that you involve the foundation's program officer or staff liaison in your outreach, if they have one. You want that program officer to be an advocate for you, not someone who feels slighted because you didn't follow protocol and went over their head.

Businesses

Volunteers can also search websites of local businesses that often have pages about their community services and interests. Their annual reports may also reveal pertinent information. And again, you can provide them with a form that lists company officers or owners with whom they might have contacts. A useful tool for volunteers to research is your local Business Journal. Most communities have a publication like this, which often carries stories about the companies in your community and shows their gross revenues and number of employees. It will also often carry articles about local business leaders.

We will talk more about involving volunteers is raising money from businesses in **Chapter Four.**

Individuals

If you engage volunteers who are familiar with the philanthropic community, you can ask them to review your list of current donors and provide helpful information about these individuals. You can also ask them to brainstorm as a group about philanthropists in the community who might be interested in your organization. Screening meetings should involve volunteers who have broad community connections and move in circles that include major philanthropists in your community. We will address how volunteers can help more with major gifts in **Chapter Five.**

Development Planning

Volunteers can be helpful with your development planning. The development committee should be intimately involved with setting goals and objectives for the plan and exploring strategies to implement the plan. We will talk more about forming a development committee later in this chapter.

Developing your case for support can also include volunteers. However, you should not expect a volunteer to write your case for support unless you have a retired development professional as a volunteer or you have one who works for another nonprofit but can devote the time to write your case, since they may not help with donor solicitation. Another effective way to involve volunteers is to test your case for support before translating it into fundraising materials. One of Linda's clients did this very effectively.

A human service organization that provided several needed community programs had just written its very first support case and was not sure if it had done an adequate job of explaining its programs and need for support. The development committee chair suggested they hold a focus group and helped develop a list of people to invite to the focus group. Some were donors to the organization, but most were not. Invitations made it clear that they would not be asked for a contribution but were invited to give advice. The case was then translated into a PowerPoint presentation. Volunteers were invited to the organization for a catered lunch buffet. After everyone had been greeted, introduced, and invited to start their lunch, the executive director thanked them for coming, explained why they were holding the focus group, and assured the volunteers that they would not be solicited for a donation. The chair of the development committee then went through the PowerPoint presentation of the case and asked for input from the group. Following are some of the questions he asked:

◆ What programs of ours were you aware of before coming to this meeting?

◆ Have you learned more about the organization after participating in this presentation?

◆ What programs that we provide do you think are especially vital to our community?

◆ Are there areas we should emphasize more or less in our case statement?

◆ Are there questions you have about our organization that were not answered in the case as presented?

◆ After hearing this case, would you contribute to our organization if asked?

The organization received some great input and strengthened its case before spending the time and money translating it into printed materials.

The Development Committee

The development committee, along with staff, leads the organization's fundraising program. This committee, however, should not consist solely of board members. Involving volunteers on the committee helps you meet your fundraising goals and provides a great training ground for prospective board members.

Finding members of committees is often easier than finding board members. Many people who are not ready to accept the fiduciary responsibilities of serving on your board might want to get involved with your organization in other capacities. You can recruit development committee members who are bankers, financial planners, attorneys, media representatives, and entrepreneurs. It will also be helpful to look for people who have served on boards or development committees of other organizations because they will be experienced in fundraising.

Recruiting a development professional from another institution, providing that organization is not a direct competitor of yours, might prove helpful. Development professionals will often choose not to actively solicit donors because it could be a real or perceived conflict of interest. However, they are often willing to assist in planning, writing, or identifying donors. For example, a university development officer could be an excellent individual to add to the fundraising committee of a human service agency whose programs and donors will not compete with the university.

Often, once a person serves on the development committee and performs well, you may want to invite them to serve on the board as positions become available. A committee position is an excellent way for you to "test the waters" with a volunteer and learn more about you before they agree to submit their name for a board position.

So, who should you recruit to serve on *your* development committee? The sample development committee chart gives you one typical structure for a development committee, but each organization will have different needs.

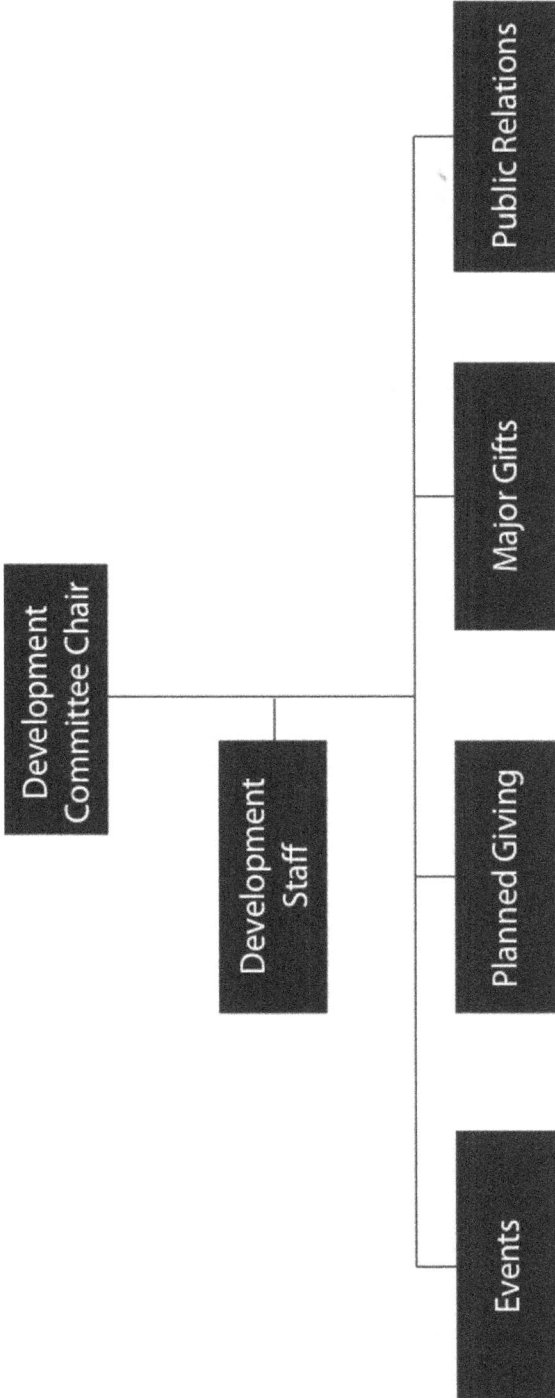

Wrapping It Up

◆ Volunteers who do not want to actively fundraise can help with researching foundations, businesses, and individuals.

◆ Get input from volunteers when developing your case for support.

◆ Unless volunteers are experienced development professionals, you probably do not want them writing grants, your case for support, or fundraising appeals.

◆ The development committee is a great way to involve volunteers who may not want the responsibility of being a board member but want to help your organization succeed in meeting its goals.

◆ Committee positions are a great "proving ground" for future board members.

Chapter Three

Involving Volunteers in Events, Direct Mail, and Phone Appeals

Your annual giving should include an event or two but do not forget mail, email, and phone appeals, which can also be part of your development plan, and all are ways to involve volunteers.

Involving Volunteers in Your Special Events

Special events are especially volunteer intensive. Most successful events have committees of a dozen or more volunteer leaders responsible for planning and implementing an event along with additional volunteers who work on specific tasks for the event. Volunteers usually serve in various capacities on special event committees, such as handling publicity for the event, making physical arrangements (e.g., booking locations), arranging for entertainment if that will be part of the event, and securing sponsors. As with any type of fundraising effort, leadership is critical to success. The special event committee chair can make or break the event. Running a major event without volunteers will be nearly impossible unless you have a full-time staff person devoted solely to special events.

Make sure you have job descriptions for each volunteer and each staff member involved in special events, so there is no confusion about roles. And be sure to debrief with volunteers after the event to assess what went right, what went wrong, and how the event can be made better next year. And ask for honest feedback—it may be time to retire some events. Who better to know this than the volunteers who worked on the event?

Involving Volunteers in Your Direct Mail Appeal

You might currently utilize volunteers to stuff mailings. You will often find that groups such as senior or youth groups are happy for an activity that helps them meet their service requirements or fill time. But volunteers can also be used in other, more meaningful ways in your direct mail appeal. Your donors are more likely to respond much better to a letter "written" by the parent of a child killed by a drunk driver, a student on a scholarship, or a recovering addict than a letter from the staff or board chair of your nonprofit. However, staff members should write the letter for the volunteer, inviting the signer's input to personalize it.

Another way you can involve volunteers effectively is to hold a focus group with potential donors and have attendees provide input into your direct mail package as it is being developed. Ask volunteers how they would respond to the carrier (outside) envelope, the letter, and any enclosures included in the package. Volunteers also can be extremely helpful in expanding and correcting your mailing list. Many times, direct mail appeals are not successful because the mailing list is not "clean." A misspelled name, an envelope addressed to a deceased or divorced spouse, or an envelope addressing someone as Mr. and Mrs. John Jones when the wife may use a different name, can be offensive for some people.

A classic example of how screening your list could prevent mistakes like this: One of the organizations Linda supported as a member has always approached her by direct mail. When she achieved ACFRE status, she sent a change of name to read, "Linda Lysakowski, ACFRE." However, when they added the ACFRE designation, they apparently thought it was part of her last name and changed her last name to Lysakowskiacfre. This took up so much space that they had to shorten her first name to "Da." So, she was suddenly known as Da Lysakowskiacfre to this agency. Guess what? She has *not* sent them any money since they started addressing her incorrectly! If the agency had a volunteer committee reviewing its mailing list, perhaps someone would have spotted and corrected this error, thus retaining her as a donor.

Use the same principles when planning and implementing an email campaign. You want to make sure that your request actually reaches its intended recipient and not end up on the spam folder or, worse, be deleted by a donor because of a silly mistake in the name.

Involving Volunteers in Your Telephone Fundraising

Volunteers can be amazingly effective in your phonathon. It is important to remember, however, that you need to provide training for these volunteers. Before the training, you will need to prepare talking points and other materials volunteers will need to be successful. Your volunteers should identify themselves right away as volunteers since many people will respond well to volunteers who give their own time, talent, and treasure. Volunteers can also be invited to participate in thankathons in which they call donors to thank them for their gifts, not to ask for money. You might want to introduce this concept to your board members as an introduction to fundraising for your organization. You might even try asking recipients of your organization's services to volunteer for your phonathon or thankathon. Who better to tell the story of why your organization is so vital to the community?

Start by recruiting a chairperson for your phonathon. This person will sign your letters to the prospective donors and help recruit team leaders for each night of the phonathon. Volunteers may even supply the use of their facilities to conduct your phonathon if you do not have the capacity at your facility. A volunteer who works at a real estate office, a stock brokerage firm, or any company with a bank of phones can provide facilities for you. Remember, volunteers will need training before they get on the phones.

There are many ways volunteers can help you better your fundraising efforts through special events, direct mail campaigns, email campaigns, and phonathons. When you utilize volunteers to help you these ways, make sure you provide the necessary training, structure, and staff support for them to be successful.

Wrapping It Up

◆ Special events are a popular way to involve fundraising volunteers.

◆ Volunteers can help review lists for mail and email appeals.

◆ Volunteers will be useful with phone appeals.

Chapter Four

Involving Volunteers in Your Annual Business Appeal

Your business appeals will be far more effective if you involve a team of volunteers to make visits to business owners or managers. An annual business appeal, done through face-to-face solicitations, is an area that many nonprofits have tried and found to be the most successful way to approach businesses. Volunteers enable your organization to reach many business leaders you may have found impossible to meet in person. These volunteers will be calling on someone they have a personal and/or a business relationship with. We talk more about this in our book, ***Nonprofit Quick Guide: How to Run an Annual Business Appeal.***

Instead of appealing to businesses through the mail, establish a peer-to-peer solicitation program. Start with one or two business leaders already involved with your organization, either serving on a committee or on the board. Select a chair and vice-chair or co-chairs who have a passion for your mission and who have already made financial commitments. These leaders will then help build a team of other businesspeople who can talk to their friends and business associates about contributions.

Determining How Many Volunteers You Need

When personally soliciting businesses, a good rule of thumb is to ask each volunteer to make no more than five visits. If volunteers are expected to make more than five calls, they will often get frustrated, feel overwhelmed, and not even make one visit. So, once you have developed a list of business prospects, this is the easy part.

To determine how many volunteers you need for your business appeal, first, make a list of all the companies you would like to solicit. Then divide that list by five. Start small! You might have hundreds of businesses in your community, but select the ones with which you think you will have the best chance of succeeding. Select companies that are involved in or connected to your organization. For example, maybe one or more of the local banks has entered teams in your golf tournament or bowlathon. You should always include your vendors. And include companies whose products have a natural connection to your mission. For example, if you work for a health care facility, plan to contact any local manufacturers of medical supplies or pharmaceuticals.

Once the program expands to what seems to be an unmanageable size, divide the volunteers into teams of five people and work with team leaders.

Back to the volunteers. Be sure to provide positions descriptions, such as those that follow, for all volunteers. Basically, you will need:

◆ A Business Appeal Chair
◆ A Business Appeal Co-Chair
◆ Business Appeal Team Leaders
◆ Business Appeal Team Members

Your volunteers will need a training session in which they will learn how to make the "case" for your organization and how to ask for a gift. If this is the first time these volunteers have been involved with an appeal of this type, they may need more intense training on topics, such as scheduling a meeting. However, if the volunteers are relatively sophisticated and will be calling on their friends and peers, they may not need as much training.

At this training, be sure to provide your volunteers with information about your organization that they can give to prospective donors. But remember, these are businesspeople, not foundation officers. They do not have the time, or perhaps even the interest, to read volumes of materials. A simple one-page fact sheet can be extremely helpful. Give the volunteers additional information, such as brochures or annual reports, for those prospects who request more detailed information.

Always begin with a kickoff meeting where you will provide your volunteers with information packets containing all the materials you have developed. Be sure to answer any questions about your organization and its programs. Provide training or a refresher in making the "ask." A key part of this kickoff meeting will be an inspirational talk. If you can invite a client who is receiving services from your organization, this talk will have an even more significant impact.

Report meetings will also be important so your volunteers can celebrate success, provide feedback on how the program is going, and receive hints from other volunteers on approaching their prospects. Sometimes these report meetings can be highly effective in motivating those volunteers who are not doing well by providing them an opportunity to hear from other volunteers who are successful with their visits. And, of course, if your volunteers have a healthy sense of competition, this might be the time to encourage some competitive interaction.

One of Linda's clients was engaged in a capital campaign. They had assembled a great team of volunteers who represented the local business community leadership, including the presidents of the four major banks in the community. At one campaign cabinet meeting, one of the bankers was boasting about a recent bank acquisition that now made his bank four times the size of his colleague's institution. The colleague very quickly responded with, "Oh good, our bank is pledging $250,000 to the campaign, so I am sure your bank will now give $1 million!"

At the end of your business appeal, plan a victory celebration for volunteers. Prizes can be given to the volunteers who have raised the most money or completed the most calls. Volunteers from the business community often are inspired by friendly competition. A staff person, board member, or volunteer might want to take on the challenge of soliciting some local restaurants and other businesses for gift certificates that can be used as prizes. Keep all meetings short and at a convenient time for businesspeople, which often is the first thing in the morning.

For more information on tapping into business motivations and giving vehicles, see our companion books, *Nonprofit Quick Guide: Best-Kept Secrets to Engaging and Retaining Business Donors* and *Nonprofit Quick Guide: How to Run an Annual Business Appeal.*

Wrapping It Up

◆ Businesses will respond better to an appeal from a peer, so business volunteers can be a compelling way to boost your fundraising from businesses

◆ Remember, when volunteers are making personal visits to businesses or individuals, the five-to-one rule is critical. Do not give them huge lists to call.

◆ Business volunteers may be more competitive than other volunteers.

Chapter Five

Involving Volunteers in Major Gifts

While there are numerous roles volunteers can play in the annual fundraising program, perhaps none is more critical than the role of identifying, cultivating, and soliciting major donors. For many donors, the person who asks them to contribute is one of the most important factors in determining the financial commitment they will make. Most people like to be asked by someone they know. A colleague or friend, sometimes even a relative, usually has much more success than a staff member.

Why Volunteers Are Effective at Making the "Ask"

One of the reasons volunteers are so good at asking for money is simply that they *are* volunteers. They are not viewed as professional solicitors whose jobs depend on raising money or as "hired guns" who may not have the donor's best interests in mind. They will come across as people with a genuine interest in the organization's mission because they have already supported this mission with contributions themselves. The main reason volunteers can be more effective than staff is that they are usually soliciting their peers and approaching people to give at the same level they have already given.

Volunteers play a critical role in major gift fundraising. They bring sincerity and commitment to the table. They usually have connections that often would not be available to you as a staff member. Their special expertise and leadership qualities lend credibility to your organization. Volunteers make good fundraisers for several reasons:

 ◆ They are not getting paid to do it, so they are not under pressure to perform.

 ◆ They have a real commitment to the mission of your organization.

◆ They have already made contributions themselves, ideally at the same level they ask prospective donors to contribute.

◆ They care enough that they are taking the time to participate in your fundraising program.

◆ They generally have strong relationships with potential donors.

How Volunteers Can Be Involved

Volunteers can help you identify prospective major donors. Often this is done during the process of screening meetings. Here is how screening meetings work, and how to choose the right volunteers to help with this activity.

Select your committee members very carefully and make them aware that the information shared in these meetings is *very confidential*. If your board or committee volunteers have never done screening before, explain to them that this method is used routinely in most organizations and is the best way to determine the key ingredients of a major gift: linkage, ability, and interest (the LAI principle). If you are working with a consultant, the consultant will generally lead the screening meeting. If you do not have a consultant, be sure that the session is led by an experienced group facilitator. It will be especially important to keep the group on task and explain the methodology and reasons behind the screening meeting to those who are not familiar with the process.

It is also crucial to start with a preliminary list. It is often hard to get a brainstorming session started with a blank slate. Prepare a list of the top 10 percent of donors to your organization or other prospects you feel may have the potential to make major gifts. List the giving history of these people, with their largest gifts and their most recent gifts. Provide a column for each of the key ingredients: linkages, ability, and interest. Be sure to mark the sheets "Highly Confidential." Gifts that have been made anonymously should not be listed.

Now to the three methods:

1. *The open screening session.* Invite the group to assemble in a quiet room. Open the discussion with a brief explanation of the process, its importance to your organization, and why they were selected to help with this task. Then distribute the lists and discuss each name on the list, attempting to determine the best linkage—who knows this person best or who would be the best person to make the "ask." There will often be several linkages, and the task of this group is to determine the best solicitation team. Next, try to assess ability. What *could* this person give to

the organization if so motivated? Without revealing confidential information, the screening committee members often can estimate the person's net worth and/or income. Then try to determine interest. Does this person have knowledge of your organization? Is your organization a cause this person is known to support? Is there a specific program of your organization or part of your project that you think would interest this individual? As each name is discussed, complete the form with the linkages, ability, and interest named. The advantage of this method is that there are discussion and consensus. The disadvantage is that some people feel uncomfortable discussing prospects.

2. *The closed session.* This method is remarkably similar to the first, except that instead of discussing each prospect among the group, participants in the session are asked to complete the answers to the linkage, ability, and interest sections to the best of their own knowledge. Each person works independently, without discussion among the group. Lists are then collected, and the person in charge reviews the lists and determines the consensus of opinion. The advantage of this method is that people may feel freer to comment on prospects if they are doing it confidentially. The disadvantage is that once the lists are collected (screeners should mark their names on the lists before turning them in), there is a lot of guesswork and perhaps follow-up to clarify what a screener has written. Without the open discussion, it is sometimes difficult to figure out why one person thought this prospect could give $1 million, and another suggested $10,000.

3. *The private screening session.* This method is similar to the first, except that it is held one on one with a staff member and a screening committee member. The list is reviewed with screening committee members, one at a time, in the privacy of their offices or homes. This method's advantages are that it is easier to schedule people at their convenience than to get them all together in one room. The open discussion takes place at least between the staff and the screening committee member. The disadvantages are that it takes a lot more staff time to meet with screening committee members individually. Again, the lack of open discussion may require follow-up to clarify significant differences of opinion.

In all three methods, you should encourage screeners to add their own names to the list. Seeing the list will often jog people's memories to think of other potential donors for your organization. Whichever method you use, you will most likely uncover some hidden "stars" among your current donors and discover new prospects along the way.

Involving Volunteers in Making the Asks

One of the things that you will uncover in the screening session is the right person or team to make each ask. Volunteers are typically good at this part because they are calling on people with whom they already have a relationship. They can open doors you may not be able to open. Even if they would prefer not to actually make the ask, they can lay the groundwork for a staff member, a board member, or another volunteer to make the ask. However, it is usually best to let volunteers make the ask for several reasons. First, they know the prospective donor and will usually read signals from the donor that this may not be the right time, or the right amount, or the right project. And they may be able to offer alternative suggestions based on the knowledge of the donor's interests and ability. Second, they are peers, so they can say, "Hey Joe, I know you believe in this cause as much as I do, and I have committed $10,000 and would like you to match my gift." Even if they are not comfortable sharing the amount of their own gifts, just letting the donor know they made a gift and want their friend or colleague to join them goes a long way.

Of course, if your volunteers are new at major gift asking, they will probably be skittish. Ways to relieve their fears include providing them with as much information as you can about the prospective donors, making sure they are comfortable explaining your case for support, and ensuring that they have made their own gift before asking others to give. The best way to assure volunteers are comfortable with asking for a major gift is to pair them up with another, more experienced volunteer, a staff member, or a board member. Joint calls are almost always more effective. You raise the volunteer's comfort level. While one person might have a relationship with the donor and feel more comfortable asking that donor to join them in supporting this case, the other person may know more about the organization or the funded program.

Of course, your volunteers will need some training, which can be done by a staff member or a consultant if you are working with one. Volunteers, as part of your major gifts team, can make a world of difference.

Wrapping It Up

◆ Volunteers are effective askers because they are usually the person most familiar with the prospective donors.

◆ Volunteers are most effective when calling on people to give at the same range they give.

◆ Volunteers can help qualify prospective donors through screening sessions.

◆ Do not forget to provide training for volunteers.

◆ Usually, the best solicitation team is a staff member and a volunteer.

Chapter Six

Involving Volunteers in Capital Campaigns

The right campaign cabinet is one of the most important indicators of whether your capital campaign will be successful or not. Involving key community leaders in your project can make all the difference in the world. Your board and staff alone should not try to run a campaign without key community leaders' support. If they do, they miss out on a lot of talent, connections, and money these community leaders can provide to your campaign.

Before recruiting people to serve on the campaign cabinet, your campaign steering committee should review a list of potential donors and try to get those with the greatest potential to give to also become involved in the campaign. A steering committee is a small group of internal staff, board members, and possibly a volunteer who is deeply involved with the organization and is expected to take a lead role in the campaign. The cabinet is more external and should be comprised of key community volunteers with influence among prospective donors for the campaign.

Where will you find volunteers for your campaign cabinet? A list of business and individual donors and a list of potential volunteers will be developed through the planning study process. This can serve as the basis for recruiting campaign leadership. It will be vital to include key community leaders in the planning study process. It is much easier to invite these leaders to serve in a campaign capacity if they have been included in the planning process.

Volunteers will also be able to expand the scope of your prospect base and will be far more effective at soliciting their peers than anyone within the organization can be on their own. They may, in fact, be the only ones who can open doors to major donors.

The Role of Volunteers in a Campaign

What will the volunteers do? You may need hundreds of volunteers to run a capital campaign. Do not panic, though; your committee chairs will help recruit volunteers for the aspect of the campaign they are heading up, so you do not have to think about recruiting hundreds of volunteers. Just recruit the right campaign cabinet, and the chairs will help you fill in the rest of the spots.

Part of your campaign plan will be to develop a list of the number of volunteers you will need with job descriptions for each volunteer victory. Starting with the campaign leadership, it will be important to find the right person to do the right job. Some volunteers will be needed for planning campaigns and events and coordinating campaign publicity. Still, most campaign volunteers will be involved in the crucial tasks of identifying, cultivating, and soliciting, and stewarding donors. It is critical to have an organization chart and position description for every volunteer job within the campaign. The following example shows how volunteers will be involved in your campaign.

CAMPAIGN VOLUNTEER POSITIONS

Committee	Positions	Number of Volunteers
Capital Campaign Cabinet	Chair	1
	Honorary Chair	1
	Chairs and Co-Chairs of Committees	14-28
Board Gifts	Chair or Co-Chairs	2
	Members	2-6
Staff Gifts	Chair or Co-Chairs	1-2
	Summer Staff Committee Members	3
Prospect Development & Evaluation	Co-Chairs	2
	Committee Members	2-3

Lead Gifts	Co-Chairs	2
	Committee Members	2-4
Major Gifts	Co-Chairs	2
	Vice-Chairs	4
	Members	8-12
Special Gifts	Co-Chairs	2
	Vice-Chairs	4
	Members	15-20
Vendor & Business	Co-Chairs	2
	Vice-Chairs	4
	Members	15-20
Organizations	Co-Chairs	2
	Members	2-3
Special Events	Co-Chairs	2
	Regional Vice-Chairs	4
	Regional Kick-Off Event Co-Chairs	4-8
	Regional Kick-Off Event Committee	20-30
	Regional Cultivation Events Co-Chairs	4-8
	Regional Cultivation Events Committee	20-30
	Dedication Event Co-Chairs	2
	Dedication Event Committee	5-7
Public Relations	Co-Chairs	2
Speakers' Bureau	Co-Chairs	2
Total Volunteers Needed		**157-224**

You may not need this many volunteers; it depends on the size and scope of your campaign. For example, if it is a local campaign, you will not need regional committees.

Where to Find Campaign Volunteers

How do you find volunteers? The planning study report is the first place to look for potential volunteers. Ask your board members, other volunteers, and staff for their suggestions about people who can help. Of course, most campaign volunteers will invite other volunteers to join their committee or somehow get involved.

Volunteer recruitment will need to be handled with extreme care. Often, organizations want to jump the gun and start recruiting campaign leadership before they have a clear idea of the expectations for these volunteers. It will be vital to have a campaign plan in place that includes, among other things, position descriptions for all volunteer roles and timelines for each committee.

Trying to fit volunteers into roles after they are recruited is like hiring a staff person and then deciding what the organization wants the person to do. The volunteer recruitment process must be handled just as carefully as one would handle hiring a staff person, with due diligence and thoughtfulness of this volunteer's best role.

The campaign plan is the foundation for a successful campaign and will help you get things off to a good start. The plan should include a brief overview of the process taken by your organization that led to the campaign. A vital ingredient of the plan is the campaign organizational chart showing all the various divisions of the campaign and the number of committee people needed to staff all the divisions. Position descriptions for all volunteers should also be included in the plan, along with a timeline for each committee and an overall time schedule.

Volunteers should not be recruited until the plan is completed. It will be critical to show your volunteers that a well-thought-out plan, including volunteers' expectations, has been developed. Hence, they understand their role and the time and monetary expectations that will be asked of volunteers. The principal groups of volunteers involved are members of the campaign cabinet, which includes chairs of all the various committees that will be involved in the campaign.

For a more detailed discussion on implementing a capital campaign, see our ***Nonprofit Quick Guide: How to Run a Successful Capital Campaign***.

Wrapping It Up

◆ A campaign cabinet of key influential community leaders will ensure that your campaign has every chance to succeed.

◆ Do not try to run a campaign using your board as the campaign cabinet.

◆ If you have done a planning study, the consultant should provide a list of prospective campaign volunteers.

◆ Know what divisions you will have in the campaign before you start recruiting volunteers so you can find the right volunteers, i.e., alumni soliciting other alumni, major gift donors soliciting other major gift prospects, business leaders soliciting other business leaders

◆ Make sure every volunteer has a job description.

◆ You might have hundreds of volunteers involved in your capital campaign.

Chapter Seven

Involving Volunteers in Planned Giving

While planned giving, because of the specialized knowledge involved, is often thought of as a role for a staff member or consultant, volunteers can be instrumental in various ways with your planned giving efforts. A committee of volunteer professional advisors can teach your staff about various planned giving instruments, develop effective promotional materials for planned giving, make connections for the organization with potential donors, and conduct planned giving seminars.

Volunteers who have already made planned gifts themselves are the best spokespeople for your organization's planned giving program. Once people have indicated that they have made planned gifts to your organization, you should invite them to help identify other potential donors and introduce them to your organization. Volunteers can also be asked to give testimonials or write articles for your newsletter about why they made planned gifts to your organization.

Some Ways Volunteers Can Help with Planned Giving

You should include some volunteers on your development committee who have expertise in planned giving and bequests. For example, estate planning attorneys, financial planners, CPAs, and insurance agents. These people will be able to do several things to help your planned giving program:

◆ Talk to your board about how planned giving works and the board's importance in leading the way by making a planned gift.

◆ Conduct wills seminars and other planned giving seminars for your donors, staff, and volunteers.

◆ Write articles about planned giving for your newsletter and website.

◆ Refer clients of theirs who might be looking for a charity to leave in their will.

Donors should always consult their own advisors when considering a planned gift but having experts to answer questions and provide information is a huge asset for your organization.

Donors who have made a planned gift themselves can also volunteer in several ways. If they are comfortable speaking at a seminar or privately to their friends about making a planned gift, you can invite them to make referrals. You can also write feature articles for your newsletter about donors who have made planned gifts.

Often funeral directors will be willing to put information about your planned giving program in their offices. Many family members will request gifts to a charity in place of flowers. Your volunteers with expertise in this area might be willing to help you develop a brochure that can be used when approaching estate professionals, such as attorneys, financial planners, and CPAs, as well as funeral homes. Once they become involved in your organization, they are likely to refer you to their colleagues who might have clients looking for a charity to leave in their will.

Most planned gifts, by the way, come in the form of bequests. Although there are many vehicles for planned giving, which is why having a planned giving subcommittee of your board, with knowledge about trusts, real estate trusts, and other planned giving vehicles, will be helpful.

Wrapping It Up

◆ Recruit a planned giving subcommittee as part of your development committee.

◆ Select people with expertise in bequests and planned giving vehicles such as CPAs, estate planning attorneys, financial planners, and so on to serve on your committee.

◆ These volunteers can write articles, help you develop a planned giving brochure, and conduct seminars on planned giving topics.

◆ They can also refer their clients and other professionals to your organization if they do not have a favorite charity of their own.

Chapter Eight

Finding, Training, and Retaining Volunteers

What qualities should a volunteer fundraiser possess?

◆ Volunteer fundraisers must have integrity to gain the trust of potential donors.
◆ Volunteer fundraisers should be good listeners.
◆ Volunteer fundraisers must care about people and be able to relate to your constituents.
◆ Volunteers who serve in leadership roles must be able to inspire and motivate others to action.

Finding Volunteer Fundraisers

If you are already involving volunteers in areas such as program or administration, you might want to begin with those volunteers who already have demonstrated a commitment to your organization. You can bring these volunteers together for a meeting to invite them to consider taking on new responsibilities in the form of fundraising. Suppose your organization has involved volunteers in minor fundraising roles, such as helping at special events or stuffing envelopes. In that case, you can ask them if they have an interest in becoming involved at a deeper level, such as soliciting prospective donors through your phone appeal, business appeal, or major-gift appeal.

Volunteer Recruitment Steps

◆ Develop a list of the volunteers you need.
◆ Develop a list of potential volunteers.

◆ Find the right person to ask each prospective volunteer.

◆ Prepare a volunteer recruitment packet that includes the position description for the volunteer task you ask them to accept.

◆ Meet face to face with prospective volunteers to discuss their volunteer commitment.

◆ Welcome and orient volunteers to your organization.

◆ Provide education and support for all volunteers, as needed.

◆ Manage the volunteer program, making sure you assign volunteers to roles appropriate for their time and talent.

◆ Acknowledge and recognize volunteers appropriately.

If you have never involved volunteers, a good place to start is with those who have already shown an interest in your organization or have ties to it. Alumni are found in many organizations, not just educational institutions. Perhaps the nonprofit has individuals who have participated in rehabilitation programs, taken art classes, or been blood donors. These are your organization's "alumni." Do not overlook them. They already know your organization and are often very committed to it.

Even animals can be "alumni." Linda once worked with a dog rescue group that was engaged in a capital campaign. They decided to run a phonathon as part of the campaign. No, the dogs did not make phone calls (although the honorary chair's adopted dog did include her paw print on the signature line of the letter that went out to potential donors). But they asked people who had adopted dogs in the year 2010, for example, to call other "parents of alumni," those who had also adopted dogs in 2010, and ask for their gifts to the campaign. Their canine "alumni" were extraordinarily successful in raising money for this campaign.

Volunteers can also be found through local businesses and service or professional organizations, many of which have formal volunteer programs. Your board, staff, and development committee can often help recruit volunteers for various fundraising roles. Local chambers of commerce are great ways to connect with businesspeople and entrepreneurs looking for opportunities to get more involved in their communities.

Many communities also have leadership programs in which community business leaders enroll to learn more about the nonprofit world with the goal of serving on the board of a nonprofit organization. These programs can be a great source of volunteers.

You also need to join the "rubber chicken circuit," speaking at meetings of local service and professional associations whose members might be able to volunteer as a group or individually.

Check to see if your community has a volunteer center that matches volunteers with organizations and performs much of the screening of volunteers. This can be another source of volunteers, although the best fundraising volunteers will be those you personally recruit who have a relationship with your organization.

Where Can You Find Volunteers for Your Development Committee?

Try the following steps to build your development committee.

◆ Determine how large you want your committee to be and what types of people you need on the committee (event planners, planned giving experts, philanthropists, etc.).

◆ Always develop a position description before talking to volunteers about serving.

◆ Decide who is going to ask these people to serve on the committee.

◆ Develop a volunteer recruitment packet that contains your case for support, your development plan (if you have one), a list of board members, the development committee position description, a list of meeting dates, and any other pertinent information about your organization.

◆ Start the recruitment process by determining the person on your board who most "gets it" about fundraising and ask that board member to chair the development committee.

◆ Ask your board for suggestions, particularly the nominating or governance committee, which may have some names of people who were suggested as board members but for one reason or another were not invited onto the board. (Be sure the reason they were not invited is not that they were deemed "unworthy" of a board position. If they are not good potential board members, they are probably not good potential development committee members. However, many of the names your committee will provide might not have been invited onto the board for other reasons and would possibly be good candidates for the development committee.)

◆ Ask your staff for suggestions. Often, they know people interested in your program and meet the requirements you have outlined in the position description for development committee members.

◆ Review your donor list and make sure you have donors on the development committee, preferably major donors.

◆ Talk to those who already volunteer for your organization in other ways, perhaps at special events or other fundraising activities. Pick the best volunteers to serve on your development committee.

◆ Use your networks through groups like the chamber of commerce, leadership programs, and service and professional clubs you belong to.

Keeping Volunteers Involved

Clearly communicate your expectations to volunteers. Provide the tools that will enable your volunteers to succeed. Acknowledge that the volunteer role is important to your organization.

While Linda was working as director of development in a nonprofit organization, preparing for its first annual business appeal, a new business leader moved into town, accepting a position as CEO of one of the area's leading companies. One of her board members suggested she talk to this individual about getting involved with their business appeal. She called and was able to schedule an appointment with him. Her next step was to put together a volunteer recruitment packet that included a job description, a timeline for the business appeal, the case for support, a list of other business leaders who had already agreed to serve on the business appeal team, a list of current board members, and some additional information about the organization. When Linda met with this CEO in his office, he indicated he had only about thirty minutes for the meeting, so after introducing herself and telling him a little about her organization, she produced the volunteer recruitment packet she had prepared for him and explained that we would like him to serve as a team leader in the business appeal. She suggested that this would be a great way for him to get to know some of the other business leaders in town. She reviewed each piece of the volunteer recruitment packet with him, answering any questions he had, and the result was that he agreed to serve as a team leader. Before Linda left his office, however, he said he wanted to tell her why he agreed. "I've been in town all of two weeks, and at least fifteen nonprofit leaders have contacted me to contribute to their cause, serve on their board, or somehow get involved with their organization. But you are the first one who came to see me so well prepared. I know exactly what you expect of me, how much of my time it will take, what the benefits to me and my company will be, and how much of a financial commitment you expect from me. So, you are the only one I said yes to." He was an excellent team leader. The following year, he chaired the business appeal. The next year, he was appointed to the board of directors. And soon, he was chair of the board. All because she went to that first meeting prepared to make the best use of his limited time, to inform him about the organization's expectations, and to listen to his expectations of the organization.

Past donors are an especially good source of volunteers. If they already have supported your organization, it will be easy for them to invite others to join them in this investment. A group of past donors could be invited to a special luncheon at which volunteer opportunities are presented.

Another way to find volunteers is to involve your staff and board members in the identification process. Once you establish volunteer needs and determine the qualities needed to fill each of these volunteer roles, you can have board and staff members brainstorm at a meeting to identify a list of potential volunteers who might have the qualities to fill these roles. Then develop a plan to select those who best meet your organization's needs and begin to recruit these volunteers.

Possible Sources of Volunteers

- ◆ Donors
- ◆ Recommendations from other volunteers
- ◆ Clients or users of services
- ◆ Service clubs—Rotary, Lions, Sertoma, Kiwanis, etc.
- ◆ Religious institutions
- ◆ Chambers of commerce
- ◆ Board members' suggestions
- ◆ Development committee suggestions
- ◆ Website visitors
- ◆ Leadership programs
- ◆ Volunteer centers
- ◆ Newsletter readers
- ◆ Staff contacts
- ◆ Businesses

◆ Senior citizen centers
◆ Universities

Recruiting Volunteers

Staff, board, or other volunteers can recruit volunteers. Asking volunteers to help you find people like themselves who share an interest in your mission is the best way to recruit additional volunteers.

Always have a position description for every volunteer position before you talk to prospective volunteers. The job description is important because volunteers want to know the expectations before committing to serve in any capacity. Job descriptions are critical for every position, from the chair of a campaign or appeal down to the researchers and phonathon callers.

Volunteers position descriptions should include the following:

◆ Overall responsibilities of volunteers.
◆ Specific tasks to be achieved by this volunteer position.
◆ Experience required or desired.
◆ Supervision provided for volunteers.
◆ Training provided for this volunteer function.
◆ The time commitment expected, including training time.
◆ The time frame for the event or appeal, including starting date, ending date, and meeting dates.

Sample Development Committee Position Description

◆ Work with appropriate staff to develop a long-range and short-range development plan.
◆ Plan and oversee all fundraising activities of the organization.
◆ Contribute financially to the organization and ensure full board participation in all campaigns and projects.
◆ Educate the full board on the theory and techniques of development programs.
◆ Encourage the participation of all board members in fundraising activities and programs.
◆ Attend all fundraising events and encourage board member attendance.
◆ Work with or assume the duties of a public relations committee.

Before approaching prospective volunteers, you need to develop volunteer recruitment packets for each volunteer function. Here are some items that should be in the packet. We include board members here because they are the premier volunteers in any organization. We go into the role of the board and recruiting board members in more detail in ***Nonprofit Quick Guide: Building a Five-star Board.***

Board Recruitment Packet	Development Committee Recruitment Packet	Fundraising Volunteer Recruitment Packet
Bylaws of the organization		
Board member position description*	Development committee member position description*	Volunteer position description*
List of board meeting dates with times and locations	List of development committee meeting dates with times and locations	List of committee meeting dates with times and locations
List of current board members	List of current development committee members and list of current board members	List of other volunteers involved in this committee or project and list of current board members
Your organization's case for support	Your organization's case for support	Your organization's case for support
Your development plan	Your development plan	
		Timeline of project or campaign on which you are asking the volunteer to work
Organization budget for the current fiscal year		
Any other information about your organization that might be helpful to the prospective board member	Any other information about your organization that might be helpful to the prospective development committee member	Any other information about your organization that might be helpful to the prospective volunteer

*Position descriptions should include term limits, general roles and responsibilities, and the volunteer's time and financial commitment levels.

Volunteer Recognition

Volunteers are golden. You want them to be successful, and you want to keep them coming back. Acknowledgment and recognition are essential. From a simple "thank you for your time, commitment, and passion" to more elaborate ways of recognizing your donors, make sure you have a plan in place before recruiting volunteers. Your plan might include an annual volunteer recognition event. Often these events are held during April National Volunteer Month. You can also give small token gifts to volunteers, such as a leather bookmark if you are with a library or literacy program—something made by your clients if that is appropriate. During a phonathon or a business appeal, you might give T-shirts, or a coffee mug with your logo, or candy. For higher-level volunteers, perhaps gift certificates for dinner or a spa might be appropriate. You can usually get gifts in kind for this purpose. For someone who has chaired a major appeal, try to make it something personal for that individual.

Wrapping It Up

◆ Volunteers can be an invaluable resource for your development program. There are many roles for volunteers in your fundraising program, including planning, research, and the important roles of identifying, cultivating, and soliciting donors.

◆ There are many sources to find volunteers, but the best volunteers will be those who already have a relationship with your organization.

◆ Volunteers need training, education, and support to be successful.

◆ Recognition of volunteers is essential to keeping them motivated and involved.

Chapter Nine

Bringing It All Together

As you can see, there are many ways you can involve volunteers in your fundraising program. We hope we have given you some new ideas to expand your ideas beyond special events and stuffing envelopes.

In our experience, we have found that most volunteers want to do meaningful work that they know really helps your organization. Like donors, volunteers want to see that they are making a difference. Show them how their work impacts your mission and allows you to serve more people. What better way to support your mission than to engage them in winning financial support for your organization?

And volunteers are the best people to recruit other volunteers. People respond to their peers. If you make their experience rewarding and fun, they will keep coming back and invite others to join them.

We have given you several ideas on where to find volunteers and how to recruit them. Do not forget to be prepared with specific job descriptions, expectations of time, skills required, supporting materials to help them complete their tasks, and plenty of recognition for their volunteer work. Without volunteers, many organizations would not deliver their services or would be limited in those services.

Be sure to match the right volunteer with the right volunteer job. Otherwise, you will lose them. Like donors, they want to know they are making a difference in their community. Show them that they are.

We hope that this book will provide you with the ability to recruit, effectively involve, and retain fundraising volunteers who will make a tremendous difference in your organization's success.

www.ingramcontent.com/pod-product-compliance
Lightning Source LLC
Chambersburg PA
CBHW071752050426
42335CB00065B/1778